# L. & N. W. R.
# WEST MIDLANDS
# ALBUM

## by

## Roger Carpenter

WILD SWAN PUBLICATIONS LTD.

*Title page:*
A close-up of No. 955 *Charles Dickens*, a Renewed Precedent, standing at the south end of Platform 1. With drivers Mills and Bowden of Camden, this engine travelled 367 miles a day, six days a week, on the 8.15 a.m. express from Euston to Manchester, covering over two million miles between 1882 and 1902. The legendary Rous Marten timed some memorable performances on this train. In this view the fluted coupling rods, introduced in 1896-97, have been burnished and the whole locomotive is in beautiful condition. No. 955 is best remembered for its part, with No. 790 *Hardwicke* in the race to the north in 1895.

## ACKNOWLEDGEMENTS

First and foremost I must thank Ted Higgs for bringing the collection of negatives to my attention, and David Spiers who helped in trying to establish the photographer and provided much background information on locomotive and train working in the Walsall area during the period concerned. Tel Talbot helped with LNWR locomotive details and gave much encouragement and advice with both volumes.

Information has been gleaned from the Stephenson Locomotive Society publication *Railways of the West Midlands, a Chronology, 1808 to 1954* and *Walsall's Stations* produced by the Walsall Local History Society. Bernard Mathews has provided information on locomotive allocations during the Edwardian era, and Everard Beauchamp, Bob Merry, Sandy Croall and Geoff Williams have also been of great assistance.

Tony Smith spent much time producing some of the enlargements for this book and also took on the task of turning my rambling manuscript into readable English.

Finally I must thank Paul Karau and June Judge for their skills in the production of this volume.

Designed by Paul Karau
Typesetting by Berkshire Publishing Services
Printed at Amadeus Press, Huddersfield

Published by
WILD SWAN PUBLICATIONS LTD.
1-3 Hagbourne Road, Didcot, Oxon, OX11 8DP

# INTRODUCTION

FOLLOWING on from my previous book, *An Edwardian Album of Great Western Passenger Classes*, featuring unpublished photographs believed to have been taken by the late Thomas Hinckley, this is the first of two volumes of LNWR subjects from the same extensive collection. These pictures were taken between 1902 and 1905, mostly in the West Midlands.

Hinckley was a platelayer on the LNWR and was based at Walsall for a number of years. One of his hobbies was photography and he appears to have taken his quarter-plate camera to work with him, recording stationary locomotives and trains, and, despite the limitations of his equipment, a few moving subjects. As with the GWR pictures, he tended to concentrate on passenger classes, although some freight and shunting engines are featured occasionally. Many of the negatives were in poor condition and needed cleaning and restoring, but the resulting prints have made the effort well worthwhile.

Pre-grouping scenes of the LNWR in the Birmingham area are comparatively rare as most photographers in the period were more interested in the main line from Euston. These two volumes provide a glimpse of the West Midlands scene in the transition period when George Whale had just succeeded Webb and the first of the new generation of locomotives were appearing. The ill-fated Webb compounds and the Ramsbottom 'Lady of the Lake' class were nearing the end of their main line duties and were rapidly being demoted to local work, to be replaced by the Precursors, the first of which was produced in 1904.

This volume covers Bescot, Walsall and Birmingham New Street stations and, I hope, will provide a pleasant change from the more well-known locations.

*Roger Carpenter*

Webb 'Jumbo' No. 868 *Condor* of the Renewed Precedent class roars past Bescot Junction at the head of a southbound express. The points to the Walsall and Burton line, diverging to the right, can just be seen beneath the locomotive.

This may well be a picture of Henry Holt, who was station master at Bescot Junction in 1900 or his successor, Thomas Benton, who was certainly in office by 1904.

# BESCOT JUNCTION

Bescot Junction station on the former Grand Junction Railway opened on 1st November 1847 when the South Staffordshire Railway (later amalgamated with the LNWR) opened its line from a temporary terminus at Walsall Bridgeman Place. There had, however, been a station at Bescot from the opening of the Grand Junction in July 1837. This was a short distance north of the present station and was known as Walsall until the South Staffs opened its line, when it was officially renamed Bescot Bridge. It finally closed in 1850 after the South Staffs had opened its Walsall station in April 1849.

A marshalling yard was established on the up side at Bescot and brought into use in 1881, further improvements carried out by the LNWR during the 1880s culminating with the opening of additional sorting sidings for the rapidly developing freight traffic from the collieries of south Staffordshire and the neighbouring Black Country, and a large eight-road locomotive depot in 1892. Even today Bescot is still one of the Midlands' important marshalling yards and retains numerous local passenger services to Birmingham, Wolverhampton, Dudley and Stechford. EMU suburban trains between Birmingham, Walsall and Wolverhampton also use the station. The loco depot is still open for diesels but the characteristic LNWR timber and iron station buildings have been replaced by BR type 'bus shelters'.

'Jumbo' No. 1528 *Frobisher*, another Renewed Precedent, stands in Bescot station at the head of a semi-fast train. The 'Jumbos' consisted of two very similar classes of 2—4—0, the main visible difference being that the Precedent class had 6 ft. 9 in. driving wheels whereas those of the Waterloo class were 6 ft. 3 in. Both classes were rebuilt by Webb during the late 1890s and the early years of this century with stronger frames and 150 psi boilers. The LNWR classified these as renewals rather than rebuilds. The nickname 'Jumbo' was bestowed on the class about 1882. Note the dumb-buffered PO wagon in the background and the low platforms, typical of many LNW stations in this period.

A Waterloo class 'Jumbo', No. 764 *Shap*, stands at the north end of the station with a Wolverhampton train. Whilst the capuchon on the chimney was a feature of several of Webb's passenger engines, especially 4–4–0s, only two 'Jumbos' were known to be so fitted. *Shap* was built in 1893 and lasted until 1926. For many years after 1900 she was allocated to Crewe North shed.

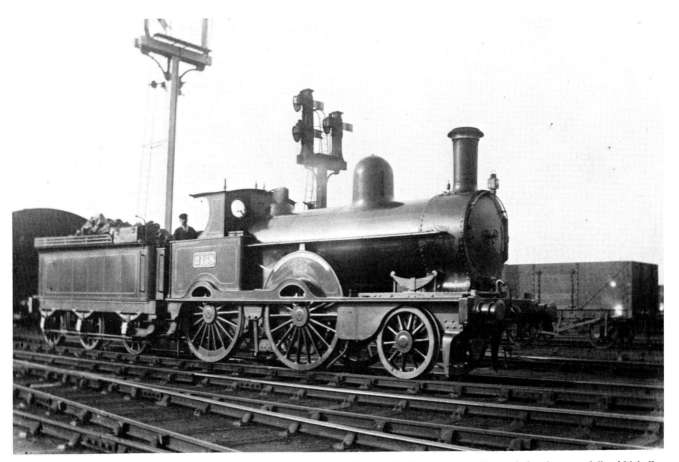

Waterloo class 'Jumbo' No. 2158 was named after Sister Dora, a greatly loved local woman who did much for the townsfolk of Walsall during the 1860s. Her work culminated in the establishment in 1868 of the cottage hospital which overlooked the railway. Among her favourite patients were local LNWR employees recovering from accidents, and in 1873 the railway staff presented her with a pony and trap as a token of their esteem, and she used this on her rounds of the streets of Walsall. She died in 1878 and a new 'Jumbo' was named after her in 1895. Mr. Webb instructed that the engine should appear at Walsall every weekday on a round trip from Derby via Birmingham. It is seen here at the south end of Bescot station on a local train to Birmingham in beautiful condition, even to the polished chimney cap.

No. 1055, a Webb four-cylinder compound 0–8–0, at rest outside Bescot running shed. Classified 'B' class, she was one of 170 engines built between 1901 and 1904. This was one of Webb's last designs before he retired in 1903 and, when Whale succeeded him, one of his first tasks was to rebuild the class as simples, although some remained as compounds until withdrawn. These locomotives were sometimes known as 'Piano Fronts' due to the ungainly front ends caused by the need to steeply incline the cylinders for clearance purposes. This shows clearly in the photograph. It would appear that the smokebox has just been cleared of ash, as the cleaner is holding a brush and his shovel stands nearby. The screw couplings were unusual for the class, and notice the double lamp sockets on the buffer beam so that it could work freight trains over the Great Central lines in the Manchester area. It is worth noting the general tidiness of the shed, including the ash pit, a contrast with latterday shed views.

*Top Right:* One of Webb's handsome 2–4–2 tanks with 5 ft 6 in driving wheels, No. 516, pauses between duties beneath the wrought iron canopy of Bescot station. One hundred and sixty engines of this class were built between 1890 and 1897. They were most successful and long-lived, forty-three remaining to be passed to BR in 1948, and the last not being withdrawn until 1955. Designed for suburban passenger work, they could be seen in all parts of the LNWR system. Many were later fitted for push-pull motor train working. No. 516 was built in May 1895, renumbered 6724 by the LMS and finally taken out of service in March 1930. Note the distinctive LNWR design of screw coupling.

*Right:* Another of Webb's suburban engines, 0–6–2 radial tank No. 938, is shown here with safety valves blowing on a northbound train. The headlamps suggest a Birmingham to Walsall express stopping at Aston and Bescot only. These 'expresses', usually worked by a Walsall engine, supplemented the normal suburban service and catered mainly for businessmen. Designed as a larger version of Webb's 0–6–2 coal tank, which had 4 ft. 3 in. driving wheels, these radial tanks had 5 ft. wheels and were commonly known as 'Watford' tanks because so many of them worked in the London area when new.

8

The ruggedness and simplicity of Ramsbottom's 0—6—0 saddle tank induced Webb to use the design as the basis of his 0—6—0 tender engine which became known as the 'coal' engine. Five hundred were built between 1873 and 1892, most of which had a long life. As a special exercise, one of these locomotives was assembled at Crewe in 25½ hours. No. 720, shown in this photograph at the north end of Bescot station, was produced in December 1880, became LMS 8214 and was finally withdrawn in September 1929. This class was used exclusively for goods and shunting work and none of the engines were ever fitted with the vacuum brake. The first batch had no brakes on the locomotive, relying on hand-operated tender brakes and the screw reversing gear, which met all the safety requirements at the time they were built.

*Top Right:* The new age in LNWR locomotive power was heralded by the introduction of Whale's Precursor class 4—4—0 in March 1904. Here No. 685 *Cossack* pauses at Bescot at the head of a Wolverhampton train shortly after entering service in October 1904. The LNW desperately needed more powerful engines for the heavier trains of the twentieth century and 130 of this class were built by 1907, quickly proving themselves and giving yeoman service into the early post-grouping period. Displaced from main line work in the early 1930s, they continued on cross-country and local passenger duties until the last was withdrawn by BR in 1949. No. 684 was renumbered 5192 by the LMS and was withdrawn in 1932.

*Right:* Following the success of the 'coal' engines, Webb produced a tank version in 1881 and built three hundred by 1896. Some were later fitted with vacuum brakes for passenger work, for which they proved most successful. Like the tender engines, the coal tanks had long lives, the last being withdrawn for preservation in 1958. No. 780 is seen here approaching Bescot with a northbound goods. This engine was built in July 1883 and is still in plain black livery. She lasted until April 1927, being cut up at Derby later in the same year.

Until after Webb's retirement the LNWR had great difficulty in providing locomotives powerful enough for their mainline expresses and the General Manager ordered that any such trains with more than seventeen vehicles must be double-headed. The problem of power shortage thus became one of engine shortage and it was not uncommon to see 0—6—0 goods engines assisting the 'Jumbos' on important expresses. Illustrated is a typical combination of the early 1900s with Problem class single No. 229 *Watt* piloting an unidentified 'Cauliflower' 0—6—0 on a Wolverhampton to Euston train through Bescot. A number of Problems were still in service at that time, piloting expresses to London and on local passenger workings.

One of Webb's controversial Dreadnought class compounds, No. 2062 *Herald*, takes on water at the south end of the station. These compounds had a bad reputation for sluggishness when starting from rest and from the early years of this century were generally restricted to local passenger services. When used on main line work, they were usually piloted by another engine. When Whale took over, they were soon scrapped and replaced by his new Precursors. No. 2062 was built in December 1885 and withdrawn in July 1905.

Special tank 0–6–0 No. 3077, designed by Ramsbotton in 1870 just prior to his retirement, rests between duties. In the ten years prior to 1880, 260 of this class were built and, although designed for shunting, some were later vacuum fitted for empty stock working. They were built with roofless cabs, unusual even in 1870, and Webb and his successors later enclosed most of them. No. 3077 was built in June 1874 as 2143, renumbered on the duplicate list in 1893, fitted with a cab roof about 1915, and withdrawn in November 1922. The damaged footplate implies that it has been involved in a minor accident. Note the driver's lunch box and the storm sheet on the tank handrail, also the disposal shovel under the rear spectacle plate.

Another of the new Precursors, No. 301 *Leviathan*, awaits the 'right-away' with a Wolverhampton train shortly after entering service in 1904. Bescot locomotive depot can be seen in the right background.

*Left:* A southbound express from the Wolverhampton direction clatters across the pointwork at the north end of the station, headed by Renewed Precedent No. 2178 *Pluck*. Bescot Junction No. 3 signal box is in the background.

Immaculate 'Jumbo' No. 2153 of the Waterloo class awaits departure at the head of a southbound train. Renewed at Crewe in June 1893 from one of the earlier Whitworths, she lasted in traffic until November 1914.

*Right:* During 1880 Webb introduced the 18 in. goods to replace the DX and coal engine classes of 0—6—0s. They had 5 ft. 2½ in. driving wheels as opposed to 4 ft. 5½ in. wheels of the coal engines and were fitted with Joy's valve gear, its first use on a railway locomotive. They were soon nicknamed 'Cauliflowers' because of the elaborate crest on the centre splashers and, although designed for main line goods work, many were later used on passenger trains after double heading was introduced. Here No. 19 stands in Besco station on a Wolverhampton express. One of a total of 310, she was withdrawn in 1943 as LMS 28508, although the last of the class out lived her for twelve years.

This view of No. 2060 *Vandal* shows the characteristic features of Webb's Dreadnought compounds. Much to the relief of the Traffic Department, most of these engines had been replaced by 1905 by the new Precursors with many of them finishing their days on local passenger trains. No. 2060 was built in 1885 and was withdrawn in July 1904.

# WALSALL

MR and LNWR engines side by side in Walsall station.

The first station at Walsall was opened on 1st November 1847 when the South Staffordshire Railway opened its line from Bescot, some 1¾ miles distant, to a temporary terminus in Bridgeman Place. This station was replaced in 1849 in anticipation of the South Staffordshire's route across the Black Country from Dudley through Walsall to Burton, running over the Midland Railway from a junction at Wichnor on the Birmingham-Derby line. The new station, opened on 9th April, was an imposing brick building and trains began to run through it to Dudley and Burton on 1st May the following year.

The South Staffs was worked by the LNWR from 1861 and was absorbed by that company in 1867.

Meanwhile, the South Staffs' first branch line, opened in February 1858 to Cannock, had been extended to Rugeley in November 1859 by the Cannock Mineral Railway, immediately leased by the LNWR.

In 1872 the LNWR began running goods and passenger trains through to Derby. Also in 1872 a direct line to Wolverhampton via Willenhall was opened, taken over by the Midland in 1876 in connection with their new route from Castle Bromwich to Wolverhampton, then under construction.

The section from a triangular junction at Castle Bromwich to Ryecroft Junction via Sutton Park was opened in July 1879 at the same time as a large Midland goods depot on the site of Walsall racecourse, adjacent to the ex-South Staffs station.

The railway map of Walsall was now complete except for the enlargement of the passenger station, completed in November 1883, and of the goods facilities in 1901. This enlarged station consisted of the South Staffs buildings and platforms adjoining Station Street with two island platforms equipped with standard timber and glass buidings. It was shared by the LNWR and the Midland, each having their own station master. In 1884 a Mr. Amatt was in charge of Midland affairs while Mr. Stevenson managed those of the LNWR.

The station booking office, built as part of the enlargement programme, was some distance from the platforms, access being by means of a long corridor of typical LNWR timber and glass design. The office itself was a lofty building of red brick, stone and wrought iron and was also shared by the two companies. It was destroyed by fire in 1916 and not replaced until the new office was opened by the LMS in 1923. This survived until the station was drastically rebuilt in 1978, entailing the demolition of most of the buildings and goods facilities and the incorporation of a new station in the Walsall shopping centre.

Except for an EMU service from Birmingham New Street, the other passenger services which radiated from Walsall have now disappeared although the line through to Rugeley is still used for goods trains. Most of the sidings are now overgrown and, apart from the commuter trains, there is very little traffic.

Buffalo Bill's Circus coach in Walsall LNWR goods yard in 1902.

'Jumbo' No. 514 *Lawrence* stands at the south end of Walsall station. This engine was renamed *Puck* in 1913 and still carried its LNWR number when withdrawn in August 1926.

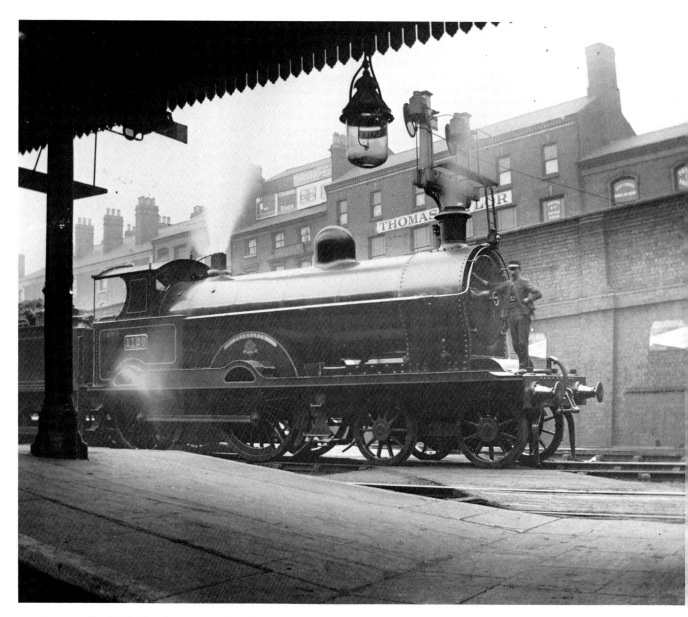

Precursor No. 1120 *Thunderer* is seen from beneath the covered way that connected the platform with the Park Street booking office. This engine is almost new, having been built in January 1905. These newly introduced 'top link' engines appeared on local passenger duties in the Walsall and Bescot districts on filling-in turns between main line duties at Birmingham New Street and Wolverhampton.

*Right:* Renewed Precedent No. 860 *Merrie Carlisle* awaits her next duty. The engine carries a Stafford shed plate, No. 14, on the rear edge of the cab roof although it was not uncommon for locos to change sheds without changing plates, especially when they had been through Crewe Works. The Park Street booking office, on the right of the picture, was opened in 1884 when the station was enlarged but was destroyed by fire in 1916. It was not replaced until 1923. In the cramped location beneath the booking hall is Walsall station signal box, while above can be seen the roof of the Alexandra Theatre.

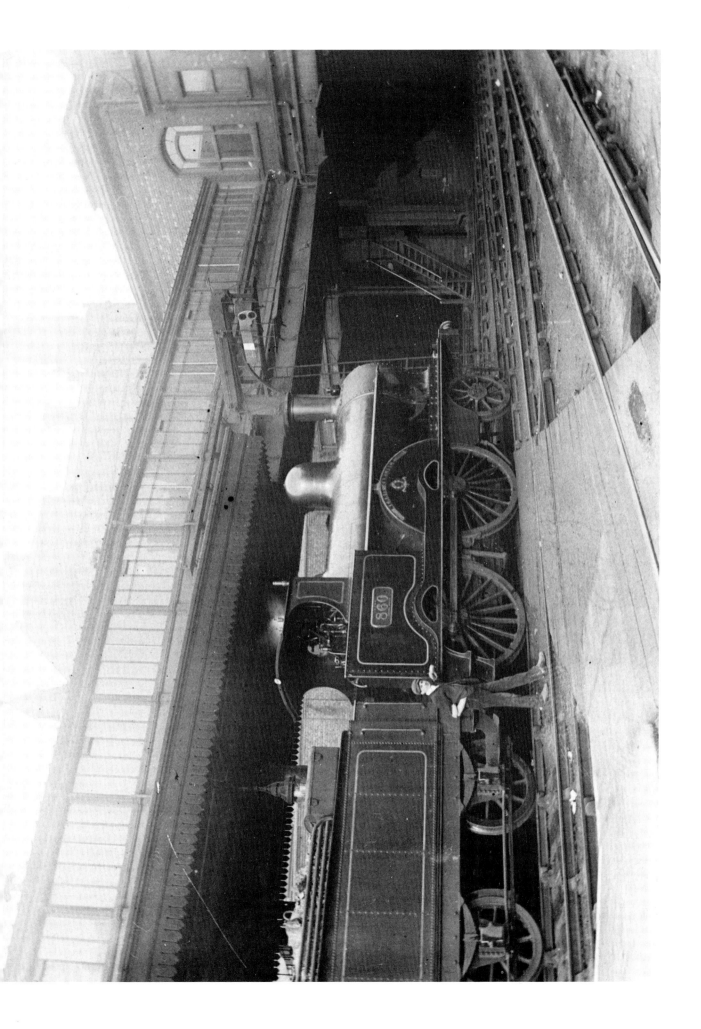

A beautifully polished Renewed Precedent No. 1685 *Gladiator* stands on a Birmingham train with the distinctive roof of one of the LNWR clerestory bicycle vans behind it. These vans, 20 of which were built in 1901-2, were popularly known as 'Boff' vans after Guard Boff who first suggested hanging cycles from hooks in the roof, thus enabling many more to be carried. With several cycle manufacturers in Birmingham at this time, these vehicles would have been a common sight in the area. Ahead of the van is Webb coal tank No. 161 which also has its safety valves blowing. The Walsall Science and Art Institute, which features in the background of this and a number of other photographs, has since been demolished.

*Top Left:* No. 1566, a Webb rebuild of the celebrated Ramsbottom DX class 0–6–0, stands beside the former South Staffordshire Railway station building. Ramsbottom built 943 of these engines at Crewe between 1858 and 1874 and Webb later rebuilt 500 of them, primarily for passenger work. They soon earned a reputation for free running and Charlewood once timed No. 1794 at 74 mph while it was assisting a 'Jumbo' on an express. By the grouping, only 88 remained and all had been withdrawn before the end of 1930, having spent their last years on local goods and shunting duties. No. 1566 was built in June 1867, renumbered on the duplicate list as 3225 in May 1909 and finally withdrawn by the LMS in December 1924.

*Left:* No. 858 *Sir Salar Jung*, a Renewed Precedent, basks in the sunshine beneath the platform covered way. Rebuilt by Webb in 1877, this engine was withdrawn in August 1912 after a comparatively short life.

Another Ramsbottom/Webb DX class 0—6—0, No. 1600, takes water between shunting duties. Built in 1867, she was rebuilt by Webb several times, renumbered 3058 on the duplicate list in April 1910 and finally scrapped in 1921.

An immaculate 18 in. goods, No. 84, stands in Platform 1 at the head of what appears to be a Derby Races excursion. Built in March 1900, she became LMS 8521, later 28521, and was withdrawn by BR in September 1949.

Webb Dreadnought compound No. 648 *Swiftsure* stands at the north end of the station shortly before being withdrawn in October 1904. She heads a local train, a duty to which many of the class had been demoted. In the background is a Johnson 0-4-4 tank No. 1277, resplendent in its red livery, at the head of an MR train. Walsall boasted two station masters, MR as well as LNWR, and had booking offices in Park Street for both companies. When these were destroyed by fire in 1916 the original South Staffs office was used until the new LMS booking office opened in 1923. Engines of the North Staffordshire Railway could also be seen at the station on a daily freight train from Stoke to the Walsall goods sidings.

*Top Right:* No. 2158 *Sister Dora* ready to leave with the daily Walsall to Derby train via the Birmingham Soho route. Note the magnificent condition of the engine with its burnished steel chimney cap, buffer heads, smokebox door wheel and handrail, and the polished brass spectacle glass rims. The large pieces of Staffordshire coal in the tender no doubt kept the fireman busy!

*Right:* The driver of 0-6-2 coal tank No. 15 poses for the camera, and the bowler-hatted gentleman on the platform is also determined to be in the picture. This photograph, though of poor quality, shows one of these long-lived and successful engines on passenger duty in the Walsall district. No. 15 was built in November 1896, transferred to the duplicate list as 3701 in August 1920, and withdrawn in October 1927 still bearing its LNWR number.

The LNWR had a small fleet of departmental locomotives for use by district engineers. The Walsall area was in the Stafford district and in this picture taken in 1902, *Engineer Stafford*, coupled to the inspection saloon, stands in the station. The engine is one of the Samson class 2—4—0s, outwardly a small version of the Waterloo class, and still retains the Ramsbottom smokebox and door. It is believed that it was withdrawn in 1923. Shortly after this time, Walsall replaced Stafford as the centre of the district.

Problem class 2—2—2 No. 754 *Ethelred* has just run round its train, probably a local from Stafford via Rugeley. These small locomotives returned to the main line at the end of the century as pilots on expresses, but after about 1904 were relegated to local services. *Ethelred* was one of the last in regular service, being withdrawn in July 1907, only four months before the class became extinct.

Set against the backdrop of the retaining wall and buildings in Station Street, Renewed Precedent No. 1744 *Magdala* takes water after bringing in a local from the Birmingham direction, while a Midland train stands in the bay behind. The Midland had their own locomotive shed at Walsall which housed a few 0—4—4 tanks and one or two 0—6—0 tender engines. They also had a fair-sized goods depot there.

Another 18 in. Goods, No. 2469, at the north end of the station. Built in November 1882, this was one of the first batch produced by Crewe in that year. Note the cast iron wheels fitted to the first ten which also originally had lower pitched boilers. This engine has rectangular section rods painted black whereas the fluted rods on No. 474 are polished. No. 2469 had a long life, being withdrawn by BR in January 1950 still carrying its LMS livery and number, 28339.

0—6—0 No. 474, an 18 in. Goods, poses with a number of staff. This engine was probably in charge of a semi-fast train, and was withdrawn in 1932 as LMS No. 8570. Note the characteristic LNWR water column. Allsop's bottle store in the background was built by the LNWR to a standard design, with a siding passing through the building.

The white diamond above the buffer beam of 'A' class three-cylinder compound 0—8—0 No. 2555 shows its train to be a fast through goods. The wagons, coal empties, are probably returning to the Cannock Chase collieries. The absence of a centre lamp socket on the buffer beam indicates that the picture was taken before 1903 when these were fitted to all LNWR locomotives. The picture is believed to have been taken in the sidings between the station and Ryecroft Junction.

Renewed Precedent No. 1526 *Drake*. Renewed in January 1890, the engine was withdrawn in August 1907.

*Left:* Ramsbottom special tank No. 3053 pauses for the camera between shunting operations, with Allsop's ale store again featured in the background. The distinctive wheel spokes show well in this picture. The large MR goods shed can be seen behind the signal on the right.

Jubilee class compound No. 1930 *Ramillies* takes water at the head
of a local train. Built in April 1900, she was one of two Jubilees
rebuilt at Crewe in 1904 with Belpaire fireboxes, the first LNWR
locos to be so fitted. This engine, like many of Webb's 4—4—0
compounds, was rebuilt as a two-cylinder simple in the Renown
class. Her Belpaire firebox was transferred to sister engine No. 1912
*Colossus* in 1921. *Ramillies* became LMS 5142 at the grouping and
was scrapped in November 1930.

*Right:* Renewed Precedent No. 477 *Caractacus* awaits departure.
The 'ghost' figure on the front is changing the lamps. In the left
background is a Midland train of close-coupled 6-wheel coaches.

The loco of a northbound train takes water while awaiting departure.
This Renewed Precedent, No. 1746 *Bevere*, also had a rather short
life, being withdrawn in July 1912.

*Right:* A Stechford train headed by Renewed Precedent No. 863
*Meteor.* This engine was another early withdrawal, being taken out
of service in October 1907. Note the LNWR platform train indicator.

The LNWR shed at Walsall, opened in October 1877, was situated in the vee of the junction at Ryecroft and replaced the 1840 shed which was nearer the station. It had twelve roads and was of the standard design of the period. Often referred to as Ryecroft because of its position, it catered for both passenger and goods engines and had a sub-shed at Dudley and a signing-on point at Hednesford. It was designed to stable 48 engines and was shed No. 9. In this view a Dreadnought compound, No. 2059 *Greyhound*, is undergoing minor repairs beneath the shear-legs. Behind the engine, which was withdrawn in February 1905, can just be seen the Walsall breakdown crane and vans.

*Right:* One of the then new Whale Precursor 4—4—0s, No. 7 *Titan*, newly built in June 1904, stands beside the coal stage in the summer sunshine. One of the Walsall shed turns was a daily return express working to Euston via Birmingham New Street with Walsall crews. The engine was probably destined to work this train, or one of the local filling-in turns already referred to. The introduction of these machines hastened the departure of the Webb compounds.

Webb Experiment class compound No. 311 *Richard Francis Roberts* at the south end of Platform 1 with a Euston express. Built in January 1884, it took the name of the LNWR solicitor who died in 1883. It was withdrawn in July 1905. It would be interesting to know if this engine was the train engine or merely a pilot, as Euston expresses by this date were

# BIRMINGHAM NEW STREET

Alfred the Great class 4—4—0 No. 1929 *Polyphemus* at the head of a northbound evening train at Platform 2. Built in April 1900, rebuilt in 1904 with a Belpaire firebox, and again as a 2-cylinder Renown in 1924, she was renumbered 5117 by the LMS and lasted in traffic until December 1930.

The first station on the present site was planned in 1846 when the Stour Valley Railway (later amalgamated with the LNWR) was authorised to open its line between Wolverhampton and Birmingham with a terminus in Navigation Street. The legal dispute over the claim by the Shrewsbury and Birmingham Railway for running powers over the line, completed by December 1851, delayed its opening for nearly two years. The S & B, by virtue of the Stour Valley Act of 1847, possessed running powers which would cease if the company were sold to or leased by any of the companies associated with the GWR. The LNWR, lessees of the Stour Valley, were determined not to allow the S & B into Birmingham and contended, quite wrongly, that the S & B had amalgamated with the GWR or were on the point of doing so. The S & B instigated a lawsuit to clarify their rights and a Chancery Court judgement of 16th December 1852 decided in their favour. After this defeat, the LNWR changed its tactics and raised all sorts of operating objections but S & B trains eventually ran into Birmingham from 4th February 1854.

The Stour Valley line had opened on 1st July 1852, the Birmingham terminus being a temporary affair with wooden platforms. In June 1854 the LNWR extended from their Curzon Street terminus which now practically abutted the SV station. This new station, with its vast roof of timber, wrought iron and glass, was the result of an agreement between the LNWR and the Midland, ownership resting with the former company and the MR paying a nominal rent and a contribution towards the working expenses.

No. 1666 *Ariadne*, a Renewed Precedent, at rest beneath the massive smoke-filled roof of Birmingham New Street station in August 1903. The locomotive was fitted with a capuchon on the chimney and, after being shedded for many years at Crewe, ended her days at Netherfield and Colwick, being finally withdrawn in September 1925.

With a through route from north to south, there was a considerable increase in traffic and the station was enlarged in the 1880s, mainly for the benefit of the Midland. A massive overall roof was built alongside that of the 1854 station, to a similar design, with a central driveway between. The earlier roof suffered severe damage during the last war and was completely removed in the late 1940s. The 1880s roof, on what was known as the 'Midland' side, survived until the station was totally rebuilt into its present form in the mid-1960s.

This 4-wheel saloon and open carriage truck are interesting examples of early LNWR rolling stock.

The distinctive lines of Webb's Alfred the Great class four-cylinder compounds are apparent in this view of No. 1923 *Agamemnon* standing in the middle road between Platforms 3 and 4. Unlike sister engines, No. 1923 was not rebuilt into the Renown class before being withdrawn in March 1925. Note the loading gauge suspended from the station roof.

One of Webb's controversial Great Britain class compounds, No. 772 *Richard Trevithick*. This, the largest class of compounds, was used on expresses from Euston to Manchester, Birmingham and Crewe. No. 772 stands in the middle road between Platforms 1 and 2 at the head of what appears to be a local train. When withdrawn in April 1906, her name was transferred to a new Precursor 4—4—0.

One of the small-wheeled Waterloo class 'Jumbos', No. 830 *Trent* is seen here coupled to a Webb Dreadnought on a southbound express alongside Platform 1. The booking office and the Queen's Hotel adjoining Stephenson Street are just visible in the background. No. 830 was withdrawn in July 1907.

Alfred the Great class No. 1979 *Nelson* at the south end of the station between Platforms 1 and 2. Built in July 1903, the penultimate member of the class, it is in practically new condition. Whale rebuilt a number of four-cylinder compounds with separate valve gear for the high and low pressure cylinders, greatly improving the efficiency of the engines. This modification was designed by Webb before his retirement. No. 1952 *Benbow* was the first to be altered and gave its name to the class. *Nelson* was not rebuilt into the Renown class and remained in original condition until withdrawn in August 1923. The No. 10 shed plate carried on the cab roof shows that the engine was allocated to Monument Lane and Aston, probably for working the heavy Manchester to Euston expresses. Note the LNWR rotating disc point signal and the gas lamps and enamel signs that were so much a part of the railway scene at that time.